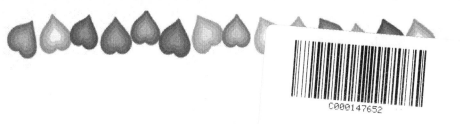

Collection of Poems
"LOVE COLOURS"

By

Samuella J. Conteh

DEDICATION

To my daughter Lindsay:

My *Window of Respite*, I cannot imagine life without you for you paint my life in alluring hues.

To my Muse:

You keep peeking from behind the curtains of my heart, amusing me and inspiring some of the poems in this collection like *Come Live In My Love, I Swear, Missing You, In Another Life, Virtual Lovers*.

To all Lovers:

Love is such a beautiful experience for all who have ever loved; or loved, lost it and loved again; or loved, lost it and never loved again.

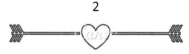

ACKNOWLEGEMENTS

Glory be to God Almighty, the giver of talents. It is only Him who could have turned all seeming impossibilities into possibilities.

M y unreserved gratitude goes to a young poet that struck the right chord in my heart for we are kindred spirits. His eye for details caught me and I convinced him to edit the poems in this collection and they came back with the most appetizing toppings. Thank you so much, Somadina Michael James of Nigeria and author of *Dance of Dandelions*: A Collection of Poems.

For a beautiful and engaging review my heartfelt thanks to Elizabeth L.A Kamara, Lecturer of Literature Head of English Unit, Language Studies Department, Fourah Bay College, University of Sierra Leone.

Lastly, but in no way the least, for the foreword I profusely thank the celebrated writer of multiple genres, Dr. Gbanabom Hallowell, Assistant Professor, William V.S. Tubman University, Liberia.

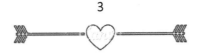

INTRODUCTION

Love Colours is a collection of poems mostly submitted for poetry contests on given themes and different poetry forms. Many of the poems featured in the collection are winning poems that have been featured in anthologies which are currently available on Amazon. Some of the anthologies that feature my poems from these contests are as follows: Eternally, Stairway to Heaven, Modern Poets, Sending Love to Mom, Bowl of Peace, Amazing Minds and Reminiscing Summer. Love Colours which is my first collection, was borne out of a desire to bring my scattered pieces under one collection.

The Author.

FOREWORD

I was in the middle of compiling a rather large anthology of short stories and poems that I had been commissioned to edit when Samuella Conteh, wanted me to do a foreword to her first collection of poems. She sent me an extraordinary collection which, I knew the author had clinically as well as extensively done, having put in long years of preparation, retreat after retreat, readings after readings; forum after forum, until she was able to discover her own voice. Such is the excitement when a poet has developed confidence to stand up and to speak for her community and for the timeless world.

I put away the anthology so as to give my best moment to reading Love Colours by Samuella Conteh. Carefully, I read through the pieces, most of which I had seen or heard her read, workshoped and developed before. I cannot help but remember her shy enduring persistent nature, even though humble and reserved. But how can one not delve in a short account of a backward-forward looking escapade beyond the collection, from its literary incubation to its out-dooring. It had all started coming together during the Sierra Leone civil war from 1991 that lasted over a decade of brutal savagery. Not that there

was anything literarily spectacular after the war, save that the resilience that people like Samuella had sustained for the honor of the nation, continued in the way that writers have supported each other in the literary growth of Sierra Leone.

The fascinating part of Samuella's literary journey is perhaps the one in which she progressively discovered friends in unexpected literary circles, even so away from outside of Sierra Leone, making her experiences, exciting enough and bold without keeping back the opportunities she had discovered. This discovery began helping her grow in the art of poetry, and in no time we began to see a leap in her daring and her confidence to conjure up and to tame imageries in a way that had never happened before. Having said the little I know about Samuella, and of our acquaintance spanning twenty years, allow me to rendezvous with the poet on the poems in the collection.

The breath of this volume speaks to its weight and to its worth. Statistically speaking, in the last five years, less than five female poets had produced a volume of poems in Sierra Leone. In five years, where there have been dozens of male poets turning out with volumes after volumes, there have only been five female poets

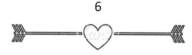

to have produced five collections. So be it, whether male or female poets, Sierra Leone is underrepresented among the countries of Africa in its literary growth even so before or after the war. Since the publication of any collection of poems by Sierra Leonean female poets beginning with Adelaide Casely-Hayford in the 1900s and then by Delphine King in the 1970s, only in the last three years did there appear one collection of poems each from Celia Thompson, Elizabeth Kamara and Princess Kailey. You can understand why literary enthusiasts in Sierra Leone have a reason to celebrate any additional female poet, as done by Samuella Conteh with her Love Colours.

> I cannot be locked in a trail
> When much my heart has to pay
> Giving much to no avail
> Sorry, now I'll have my say

In the collection, there are times overwhelming forces push and pull the central figure persona, as in the poem "Escape" or as in "If You Ever Change Your Mind" or as in "Trapped" or like when circumstances seem to break the persona down to the point where she has to resolve that "I Am Not Going to Cry." The self is always conscious and that is the strongest will that remains unwavering right through the collection.

In the end, the hand of the practiced poet consumed by fire, she goes through the crucibles on the corridors of her country's silence and it paid off as a harvest of Love Colours. Reading through the collection, one is able to see several images of colours of love, happiness, unspoken pain, kiss, memories, courage, flowers, journey and tears. Love Colours is at once an adventure into rainbows. From cover to cover, the reader is inundated with a firmament of imageries whereby the central metaphor of love remains a strong breed into which words are the fragrance, into which there's no escape, into which there's only more love.

Gbanabom Hallowell, PhD
Assistant Professor
Language & Literature Department
College of Arts & Sciences
William V.S. Tubman University
Harper, Liberia

LET LOVE FLOW

A REVIEW OF *LOVE COLOURS*

The literary landscape in Sierra Leone is glowing brighter with each passing day. We not only have more women composing and performing poetry, we also have a new breed of women who have written collections of poems. And the number is growing. Samuella Conteh, fondly called Mama Poetry because of her proficiency in composing poetry, belongs to this new breed of Sierra Leonean female writers who have published collections of poetry. Conteh has honed her poetry writing skills over the years and has been honoured with many national and international poetry awards. I count it a privilege to write a review for her and readers will agree with me that it is a joy to read her poems.

Love Colours is an enchanting piece that unveils and captures the diverse strands of love from the pen of a woman who possesses the ability to freeze intense experiences and serve them to us in poetic forms that make us pine for more. The poems in this collection are personal and at once universal. They explore the most basic human emotion, love.

This collection can be read as a voyage into the heart of a woman who has experienced both the pure bliss and agony of love – perhaps in equal measure. Within the

9

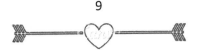

frame of love poetry, Conteh delves into themes of pain, bitterness, betrayal, deception, uncertainty, infidelity, nostalgia, courage, identity and fortitude.

Most of her poems fall within four key clusters: the sweet and tender or passionate love of lovers; illicit love relationships; the pain, bitterness and betrayal experienced by lovers; and lovers who have just discovered their identities. Men and women who have blood coursing through their veins will delight in reading these poems and wonder how someone can describe their unique situations so powerfully.

Conteh's poems are brief, unpretentious, and potent. She finds pleasure in ordering her poems in stanzas, employing lines that rhyme and using effective imagery. What is striking about her poetry is the fact that she succeeds in conveying both passionate and joyless love with such charm and authority. In *"Trapped"* for instance the persona finds herself in a world where she is:

Tossed about like a broken doll
Ripped inside out, left in tangles
Trapped, with a defeated spirit
Punctured pride lay abandoned
Restless like a ghost in distress
Lost in a graveyard of promises

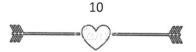

Those who have experienced disequilibrium of power in love affairs have often found themselves trapped like the persona in the above lines and until they find their soulmates – and there are soulmates for every one of us – happiness will continue to be a mirage.

Conteh's love poems in which the personae discover their identities and assert themselves   are some of the pure gems in this bewitching collection. In these poems, the personae's unfulfilled dreams and cheerless love, make them wary of love and eventually learn to affirm their individualities. *"Only As Much"*, *"Test not my love"*, *"I am not going to cry"*, *"When I fall in Love"*, *"I'm Gonna Live"*, *"Phenomenal Me"*, *"Even the Dead Gets Flowers"*, *"My New Screensaver"* belong to this group of poems that deal with women being empowered enough to discover themselves, establish the rules of the game and either say no to male dominance or channel all their energies into reshaping or rewriting their stories for themselves. This is underscored in the closing poem *"My New Screensaver"* where the persona chooses to be happy in spite of her challenges and rewrites her story thus:

> *Recharging life, overwriting sadness*
>
> *Converting full stops to smart pauses*
>
> *Editing impossibilities to possibilities*
>
> *Deleting files on failures and self-loath*
>
> *Surfing waves with a renewed resolve*

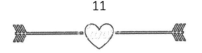

> *Painting mirth into empty fields*
> *Embracing popups of victorious songs*

How I wish people who find themselves in unhealthy situations can turn their lives around in this way. The preponderance of the continuous verbs at the start of the lines above demonstrate that the persona is determined to move forward with her life. The diction 'recharging' for instance evokes a picture of restoration or resurrection after death or near-death. There is no holding the persona back now. How far she has come!

The crown of the love poems in this debut collection is *"Love That is Evergreen"*, a poem that is highly charged with sexual imagery. In this erotic poem, the persona confesses her love for her lover using language that leaves nothing to the imagination. In simple but compelling language the persona asserts that the dewdrops of her lover's evergreen love have moisturized her, given her a new lease of life and made her think:"of making your body my shrine/to offer myself/to your naked desires".

Those who have been in highly passionate and fulfilled relationships can identify with this lover-poet whose cup is running over with love.

Conteh's poems are very captivating, down to earth and reader friendly. Lovers all over the world can identify with them and university students will find in them poems that

12

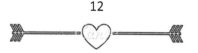

are worthy of study. In *Love Colours*, Conteh has shown that she is a highly skilled poet who has the power to charm her way into our hearts and souls and win us for poetry.

Elizabeth L.A Kamara,
Head of English Unit,
Language Studies Department,
Fourah Bay College,
University of Sierra Leone
& author of
To Cross for a Daughter and Other Poems.

13

TABLE OF CONTENTS

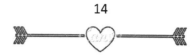

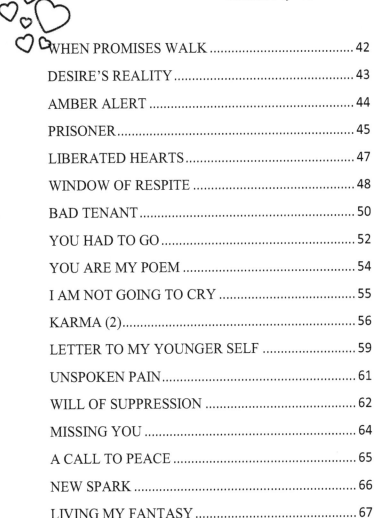

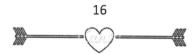

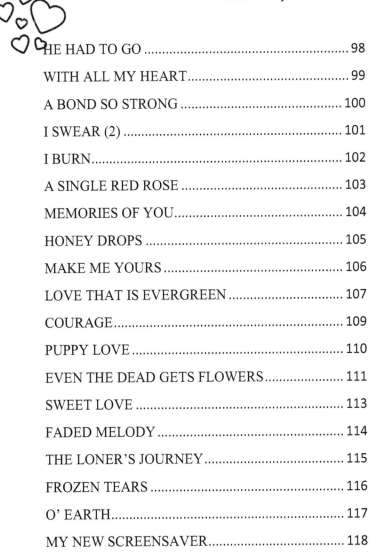

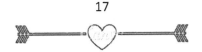

LOVE COLOURS

If love was purple
depicting royalty,
would it only be terraced
for affluence and influence
dooming folks
destined for simplicity?

If it were powdery blue
wearing the mark of innocence,
of trusting babies and virgins
would giants and old folks
die of boredom?

If it were shining white
seemingly pure,
then saints and sages
would banish sinners
into lives of drudgery

If love were red and flaming
as sung of roses,

with youthful freshness
would blood from love bruises
lose its redness?

What if it were black
shielding thoughts, dark
and intentions wack
chewing away at elation
in the comfort and promise
of a black maiden's temptation?

If it were green
smelling fresh
and looking lush,
would it turn dreary brown
when the weather, with a frown
gives it a lash till it's down?

If it were grey,
would it be somber
like angry skies
heralding thunder
and naughty rain drops?

20

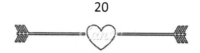

What if love
at birth was colorless
like morning dew,
would lovers grope aimlessly
in dark alleys
till fancy meets its demise?

THE FINAL DANCE

It was no party of sorts

But there was music of the sort

Its rhythm, our kind could not ignore

In a mood of celebrating your figure

My body tuned in to youthful memories

Jogging yours along like scanty Februaries

Watchers dismissed into oblivion

For us to mind together, our position

The music was perchance

Silent promises during the dance

Which exists still in Neverlands

No more dances

Sans these dreams

For there would be no party of the sort

Only music of stellar sorts

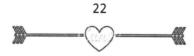

ESCAPE

We are leaving town
My aching heart and I
Destination unknown
But escape is sure

> Away from preying players
> And soul slayers
> Who nakedly clad themselves
> In well-groomed lies

I flee with my heart in tow
Away from fleeting tides of love

My stubborn trusting heart
Turned victim of scheme and treachery

> We are going away to faraway lands
> Where betrayal, on us would never lay hands
> No bitter memories taunt us for coins and cheap ranks

It's a long way to nothingness
To drown this emptiness

We might return in the light of dawn
Or while your dream is not withdrawn

Or maybe not

IF YOU EVER CHANGE YOUR MIND

Stolen moments we would ever cherish
For we have lived only for those times
Since your eyes lit mine in a spark of desire
And in that single magical moment in time
The world stood still and smiled along with us

In each other's arms, we'd learnt to let go
Shelving away the cares of our other lives
We got to moving around on wheels of longings
With knowing smiles through each day's hurdles
Just waiting for those precious times together

We can't deny this affair has been a lifebuoy
From the monotonous drift our lives had taken
It has spiced our zest for chasing a life of joy
But just like you, I also have those few moments
When I shiver between the folds of guilt

I promise I'm not going to cry, at least not now
I'll step away from the beauty of our love

But if you ever change your mind about us

I'll be right here waiting for your warmth

For I'll be frequenting this zone for a long time

DANCE FOR TWO

Stop going round in circles
I'm getting dizzy just watching
I ain't taking another sip
From this glass of uncertainty
Till I know how far you'd go

I need to hear you say it loud
That you'll dance to the end

Move away from the shadows
It's getting blurry just watching
I ain't dancing one more step
On this revolving dance floor
Till I know how far you'd go

Let me feel your heart against mine
As you tell me you are ready for us

Stop swinging with the crowd
Come sing our song with me
As we dance this dance for two

27

You know how much I'm into you
But you're picking wrong vibes

Step away from that rowdy crowd
And join me in this dance for two

COME LIVE IN MY LOVE

Starry eyed, you stall
Bewildered
At the threshold
Of my heart, waiting

Do I mean you?
What's the price?
What if, what?
So many questions

Close the door on doubt
Step into bliss that is pure
Outside of artificial grandeur
Into my natural habitat

Here, serenity beckons
I dare you come live in my love

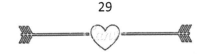

TRAPPED

Tossed about like a broken doll
Ripped inside out, left in tangles
Trapped, with a defeated spirit
Punctured pride lay abandoned

Restless like a ghost in distress
Lost in a graveyard of promises
Her mouth turns a broken loom
Spinning a yarn of woes
Dyed loss in painful hues

Would she rise or rot in self pity
Would she survive or drown
In inner strife, with no respite
To survive, is to build a resolve
To drown, is losing hope after all

THAT TIME

My lips tremble in remembrance of your kiss
Truly divine was your lusty passionate voice
With sweet promises we'd stay together forever
Cuddling in the cool of the morning breeze
That time, we were so unconditionally in love

That time, we were so unconditionally in love
Giggling as we watched the sun close its curtain
Like Siamese twins, we would cling together
Watching the cheeky moon's first playful peep
Our love was sweet and we two were a perfect fit

Cuddling in the cool of the morning breeze
Listening to trickling remnants of last night's rain
Tickling our passions to rise one more time
Each moment spent together was pure bliss
We couldn't help hugging and sharing many a kiss

With sweet promises we said forever
Believing no one would come between us ever
A day would find us apart never

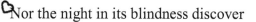

Nor the night in its blindness discover

For we were the other's half, we completed each other

For all times and in every season till forever

Truly divine was your lusty, passionate voice

Urging me to believe I was all you ever wanted

We needed nothing more for we had everything

A friend, a lover, a soulmate as heaven designed

And I'm still lost as to when the cracks began

My lips tremble in remembrance of your kiss

Before your love seeped through the cracks

To someone new hiding in your shadow's behind

Taking some of what used to be so all mine

And you're no longer in my heart's depth, mine

MISSING US

Those memories come floating along
The blue sea drinking my blue tears
They remind me how much I miss us
Like I'd ever forget how I loved you
I can't even pretend I'll ever forget
And I wonder if you ever miss me too

Do ever remember for a striking moment
Our favourite spots, couple songs
Now my single soul torment
Hopes and dreams we once shared
Do you hope to birth them with her too?
Everyone says you worship her now
Still I wonder if you ever miss us too

My ears still ring with those words
You always so sweetly whispered
How could you forget them so soon?
Even forever would never be enough
To cherish and miss what we'd had
But do you ever miss us like I do?

Everyone is talking about you and her
No one remembers I once was your all
How could you have hurt me so badly?
Pushing me off like you'd never cared
No one cares that I'm bleeding inside
Still I hope you would miss us like I do

SO WRONG FOR ME

Drifting along your selfish longings
They were left gasping for air, my affections
Losing hold of my floating emotions
While on too much laziness, you laze
Too content even for a well fed cat, you graze
So right for you, you so wrong for me

I had danced like a firefly to your light
Flapping wings of joy into your lure
Drinking in your supposed affections
Your love hinged on my purse's collections
A burden laden with too much care
So right for you, you so wrong for me

I am kissing them away, those happy times
Letting them sink down my memories' isles
Mending my broken wings again to fly
Leaving you hoping I'll change my mind
But that's a long wait to end, eternity
For you're so perfectly wrong for me

TAKING A CHANCE

The universe paused in silence
As two hearts struck a rhythm
A tightening grip at their fineness
Prying eyes watched, unseeing
Two heartstrings tied the knot of essence
Edging to sensual resplendence

Sweet tunes of harmony
Teasing their lips with a melody
Clumsy steps and wrong twists
They glided to a warm embrace
From a clouded glass sipping love's grace
A chance unlikely, floats in lovers' mist

LUSTFUL MUSING

She had seen him and thought
He looked just like a Greek god
Who'd spent time lifting weights

They had spoken and she thought
She could go to sleep warring with her guns
That was so caressingly sweet

By his musing, she's left without traces
On to very distant places
In the splendor of fant'syland

Then she saw them, his fingers
Thoughts trigger
Her heart paused as he further unraveled
Her mystery lanes

Then she felt covetous
Of those keys in black and white, she got jealous
If only the miles would go away

ONLY AS MUCH

I have since grown up, away
From that place of weakness
Tents of eagerness to run love's relay
Yearning for someone in my meekness
To love me through every nook
Thinking that was all it took

I'd fallen in love in the truest ways
Wishing it would last forever
Holding nothing back, including my days
Devotedly, I watched my passions smoldered
All I had I sent to the embers
Those jocular Junes and funny Novembers

Now my heart has a new need
Love those who of love starves and stifles
Once I never favoured greed
I only wanted to feel love's nipples
In blessed memory of the younger me
Who sans wisdom, wished for what never was

When I do fall in love again
If I ever get to believe in love ever
I'll see to it that we both gain
For the better, yes, for worse, never
Going both ways or none at all
I won't leave out the list of everything I want

All my cards, I'm pulling out
Out in the open, I'm laying them
When I do fall my back without
I'd write to love, all I need is a pen
Giving only as much as I get
Backing out when it turns a bet

Again I ain't gonna be cheated
Ain't gonna be another free ride
I'll only be as much as is needed
I've waited to be the perfect bride
So now I'll give just as much
Never too much, only as much

HAPPY ME

Behind these dazed eyes, a flood gathers
My pounding heart, sounds of mighty waters
Stupefied, I'm left standing here like a log, overdue
Watching you walk away and now I'm blue
Lovelorn and forlorn like a stray puppy
It seems my love was ne'er your hobby

I had dreamed of bright lights and mystic sounds
Faces and places I'd only seen in your eyes
But you'd prefer I go there with another
And give up all I've ever held dear for one newer
It's true with you around, I was happier
Now I choose to return to her, happy me

TEST NOT MY LOVE

You weighed my love on a scale
Hoping to read in its sway
You're so poised to get a fail
For I'm done playing that way

I cannot be locked in a trail
When much my heart has to pay
Giving much to no avail
Sorry, now I'll have my say

Measuring love as if for sale
Holding back if not done your way
Sulking when love fell too frail
For yours too was put to weigh

WHEN PROMISES WALK

A promise to stay
On the beautiful greens
That Eden was
In sweet innocence
Pure like dew
Before it touches dirt
Undressing raw desires

A promise to stay
Clothed in secrets
Of ignorance
None to tell
The serpentine gift
Of craftiness
Unveiling knowledge

DESIRE'S REALITY

A hug never promised heaven
As sweet as what we savored

My heart's song was different
From when we hugged as friends

The lyrics rang differently this time
Pulsating two bodies to surrender

Overwhelmed by mad sensations
Ringing sweeter than our imaginations

To heavenly heights close enough
Common sense beat to nought

Then the fall at the edge of desire's intensity
Back to the dreary road of reality

# AMBER ALERT

His every word
>Reeks raw anguish
>Twisting his wanton heart
>Till it drips the blood
>Of his inner torment

Her heart is locked
>Against his desire
>To possess her love
>Her eyes blind
>To his silent cry

Does she long for another?
>Has another left her numb?
>Is it a ploy to see how far he'd go?

Dear little bird take a message to her
>Whisper in her ear
>*The heart of another*
>*Is dying this minute*
>*To be saved by just three words*
>*'I love you'*

PRISONER

A lone traveler
Roams streets of despair
Pauses on bleeding soles

On bended knees
She faces the heavens
Amidst the candor of a thousand stars
Hoping their glares held a miracle

Strange

She's traversed these tracks before
Stranger still
She is still craving for love

On the journey of love
She's being hurt
Trampled
Tossed
Scarred

Strange

She's still hoping

Stranger still

She is a prisoner of love

LIBERATED HEARTS

At last
Love touches love
Hope finds light
In fulfillment of yearnings
That never subsided with the tides

At last
Love is free
To explore its wanton desires
To love and be loved
As two hearts unite

Today
One heart beats a rhythm
Only one heart fathoms
Ignoring the silent fear
"How long will forever last?"

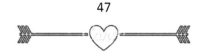

WINDOW OF RESPITE

Foundations of mansions
Fettered by a woman's sweat
For her future to abide

Dainty fingers
Scraped and sculptured
Fetched and fenced

The sacrifice of self
In the hollow of her dawn
For the night to bring her prize

The evening breeze
Slapped her face
And wrenched away her prize

She planted flowers
Pruned prided glow
With the tenderness of love

In the season of bloom

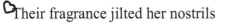

Their fragrance jilted her nostrils
While she clutched at the dew
From their last romance
She was doomed

She painted her rainbow
And adorned the stars
With pretty ribbons

Cruel dark clouds
Shot into her rainbow
Leaving her tear dam burst

From one little window
She peeped at happiness
When the rising sun
Illuminated right into her corner

Her one little rainbow
Spoke hope
Of curling laughter
Right through
Her one opened window

BAD TENANT

Love don't live here

Not anymore

A clumsy tenant

Ever the worst to see

A waster

A slob

A restless wanderer

Who wandered too far

For too long

From home

From itself

From a thousand promises

Love don't live here

Not anymore

A lousy tenant

A sorry sight to see

Too much baggage

Under-resourced

Hopeless philanderer

Who flouted every rule

A bogie man

Soggy-shoed

Booed and shooed

After a hundred changes

YOU HAD TO GO

Lost in your deceitful hugs
Stifled in a deadly clutch
Of love

A devil's whim of destruction

Enslaved
In the human struggle
To find
And be found
To keep
And be kept

Lost
In a primitive desire
To possess
And be possessed

Love turned deadly
A potential weapon
To take me out

So you had to go

For me to find myself

Again

YOU ARE MY POEM

Like a lightening bolt flashes
Through the window of my being

The garden on the hill
Exhaling such sensual perfume

A song to a heart
Crippled by desire for forever

Emotions sketched
On the canvas of my longing heart

You are my poem
Written description of my wills and woes

I AM NOT GOING TO CRY

I stand at the same crossroads
In all familiar scenes
Even the wind hisses at me now
As I stand shuffling my feet, alone
I have lost my way again
But I am not going to cry

The trees shake their branches
To laugh at my face
Dry twigs fall on my head
As I try to cover my ears
From the teasing songs of the birds
But I am not going to cry

I have crossed this bridge of hurt
One too many a time
My heart screams out its pain
But all have gone deaf to its pleas
I am weary of getting lost
But I am not going to cry

55

KARMA (2)

Dear blanket ever near
When the cold was much to bear
She wished to be bundled
Cuddled, tickled, fondled

Shortly, you turned in scorn
Blanket you dared to burn
But smoke gets into your eyes
Karma called, so your tears

I SWEAR (1)

If I can fly on the wings of memory
I would be the most beautiful thought
Lodged permanently in your heart
And be the reason you smile all day
I swear I would, if only you'd let me in

If I can fly under the belly of an eagle
I would reach right to the skies
To hide a glow behind your star
To keep your light shining so bright
I swear I would, if you'd let me hold you

If I can fly under the skirts of the wind
I would blow you love and tenderness
To put a permanent spring to your feet
And give you a cheer of silver sparkles
I swear I would, if only you'd let me

If I can fly daily alongside your steps
I would guide your feet from tripping
Keep you firm, steady and ready

To face the uncertainties of the day

I swear I would, if you'd keep me close

LETTER TO MY YOUNGER SELF

Dear younger me
How unfair I have been with you
Trumpeting my perseverance
On hauls along rugged paths
And rides on the backs of harsh tides
Daily surviving on lean meats of rejection
And losing my skin to a low self esteem

I dared to forget
It was the challenges you had to bear
That molded this better me
I can proudly project in the face of distraction
Even vainly attempting to love this older me
Than the younger me that danced on spikes

On your memories
I put a crown for all those battles won
Here's a golden shield for holding on
At the frontline of many a battle ground
This older, better and resilient me

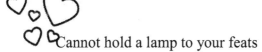

Cannot hold a lamp to your feats

So I atone by holding you well esteemed

UNSPOKEN PAIN

If we were to only paint our muses
From those images on our walls
Then voices muffled in prisons
Without walls would perish

If we could only see tears spilled
In voices of our own tongues
Who would paint hues of tears
That flow in unspoken pain

If we were to freeze our ink
In the drought of human hearts
Tears of desolation caged in hunger
Would die a voiceless death

Humanity has no race, colour or creed
Except as distinguished in man's greed

WILL OF SUPPRESSION

A mother's wailing voice rang
across the Sahara and beyond
Echoing pain that's worst
than pangs of childbirth
To see one of her own
Welding whims of hate
like an evil twin in bygone era

Sons separated at birth, flung
into the harsh world of foster care
while the mother's still breathing,
refusing to see the other as equal
but dare celebrate their coming off age

French brother still sucks on bile
spat in his mouth in oppression
Still high on dope of colonization,
he weilds the will of suppression
bequeathed him in foster care

His mind's still fettered in slavery

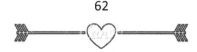

So he hurts his own sibling
feigning superiority over his brother
hurling his kith howling into forests
and strange paths in foreign fields

His image is still enslaved
like his oppressed brother
and his humanity lessens
as he kills with glee

Mama Africa weeps
for you war not
for her lullabies sang to you
while she carried your pregnancy
but for the voice of those slavers
who once held her voice captive

Harken unto the cries
of defenseless men and women
and children languishing
in refugee camps with the remains
of their stolen childhood

MISSING YOU

It's a long way to forgetting you

Lodged in my mind forever

My ears drum your voice daily

Your touch is carved on my skin

A CALL TO PEACE

On many days, I pinched myself sore
To recall my heart from the past
Many nights, I cried my heart hoarse
Mourning another love gone sour

Shaking out from dust, rightly awakened
Where it had hit, I gave a pounding
Sober realization that I'd awakened
From one too many a numbing love
I called myself to peace and self love

NEW SPARK

A warning flashes on the screen
Telling there's danger beyond the sea
Emotions slide on an ebbing tides
Numbing sensations send chills
Push button to indifferent mode
Emotionless, wearing icy stares as robe

A gently hand soothes the cold
Thaws away chunks of distrust
Putting sparks to dying embers
To ignite feelings left to freeze
Passion drives on a new leash
To breathe life into a dying heart

LIVING MY FANTASY

There's no denying my heart yearns

In yarns of desire for a love so wrong

Wrung in when we were only just pals

Playing childish games till love struck

Stuck in love, I travel years back in time

Sometimes to the freshness of bloom

Grooming my fantasies in Mills and Boon

Borne in travels to lands built in minds

I blame a note played in the wrong key

Cueing tunes sounding as sweet as sin

Since love turned the chords of a heart

Aches a heart already given to another

67

Farther into the web of our uncertainty

Tainting my loyalty to one so deserving

Serving love I could only have dreamed

Seemingly now betrayed by my fantasy

SELF DISCOVERY

Countless hours were dreamed away
At the azure sky above the flowery glade
Unhinged by all that bound her within
The future unfolds within its wraps

Stern warnings, her heart dispelled
That sad uncertainties adorned the path
Truth held more than the eyes beheld
Patience, they said will steady her gait

Above the window, her dreams grew
Restless teenage curiosity, she dared
Those childhood dreams held in tow
To find herself, her young heart willed

IN ANOTHER LIFE

Every moment I have spent with you
Has had me feeling this is all not new
A distinct echo right from the past
Like we've been on a similar movie cast
Or in some other place in another life

Never alone, always in a crowd
Till instinct drove us into seclusion
Something you said rang so close
Like you had said the same before
In some other place in another life

Each time I hear your smoky voice
I get familiarly thrilled with wonder
Where in time have I heard that sound
What were we then, one to the other
In some other place in another life

In my heart and soul I truly believe
If I hear your voice or feel your skin
Through all the years unto eternity

I will still feel like we have met before

In some other place in another life

CAUGHT IN THE MIDDLE

My heart races to yours
Even when I would rather it not
So here I am
Caught in the middle
Of wanting you so much
It hurts
My better side tells me
I should not
So here I am
Caught in the middle
Of damning what's right
To savor this beautiful sin

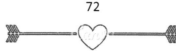

FLY AWAY

My love, I dare not look into your eyes
For I care not that you read the pain
Inked so deep, no smile can disguise
So my company will not be your gain

Today, I had to run away from his lies
His cheating, I can no longer entertain
Each time he does, a piece of me dies
And my sanity I struggle to maintain

My dear little birdie, I wish I could rise
From this love that has turned my bane
And fly away with you high to the skies
If truly my sanity I wish to maintain

PAIN

I saw the blinding colours of pain on a mother's face

Painting pictures of horror seen in wars and famine's lace

A raving beauty faded in contours of hopelessness

Eyes that once dazzled in illuminating girlish blessedness

Now lay sunken deep in sockets of untold sorrow

I heard the loud sounds of pain in the silent cries

Her only light, the glare of sadness in her eyes

And in stillness broken in bone padded shoulders

The only succor for the babies tucked inside her folders

As she listens to the rumblings of hungry stomachs

INFIDELITY

Little foxes gnaw at slender vines

of promises made at tender times

broken vows fire simmering discord

infidelity unsuspectingly ruins the record

in a rude awakening

planned or unplanned

cheating is distrust at hand

ON CAMERA

Fraught in the hands of goodbye
A last kiss before the train moves
The camera caught that last kiss
But not those stubborn salty tears
Rolling down our locked cheeks

Time, they say flies in happy times
So it would take all of eternity
Till we meet again, kiss and hug
I will stay with you in my heart
So our happy moments would ne'er depart

One last squeeze of her hands
The camera caught
But not the trembling of our hands
I will go along with you in my heart
So our happy moments need not fly

KILLING ME

You want my love without me
Working that out is killing me

You desire my heart without me
Understanding that is killing me

You want my light in the dark
Being a shadow of a lamp
That's killing me

You want my trust
With her in the middle
Living in your lies is killing me

We are both at the crossroads
And my indecision is killing me

DEAR LITTLE HEART

Keep quiet, dear little heart
We are deep in this together
Only beat for us to stay alive
Not so we welcome a stranger
Whose heart is held in trust
You know that lasts only a while
Like a quick romp in the hay
And we are left in bloody tears
So be quiet, beat for none but us

LIFE (3)

If life ever becomes a whirlpool
Swirling so fast, you lose your steam and cool
Stunned by so many possibilities
Twirling bright in hues' disparities
Pause, think before you succumb

If any seems too good to be true
Then that might just be what it is
Too good for you not to think deep
Before like a magnet, you get pulled to the steep
Observe, and pray before you let go

If life spins you on a merry-go-round
And you feel like a tiny marble, for nowhere bound
Just believe you are that right size
For the perfect fix, so find you and rise
Get inspired, to be the best of you

KISS LOVE GOODBYE

Naivety used to hold her all bound
Struggling within a heart longing to be found
To have one to keep her as his own
Chickenhearted, she fed on crumbs, per time a bone
Sipping dewdrops to calm her thirst

Just like a body without its soul
Like a ship out of steam, she drifted so
On every should, she saw respite
In every smile, a glow in spite
Of all that glared at her face, a dread of being alone

Love weary, she paused for a while
Beckoning her soul back to its fold
With a resolve that gets even stronger and bold
To kiss love goodbye on the road
When it's fondness for her grew old

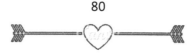

BROKEN

I might have cried myself a stream
A stream of tears, for a dead dream
We had dreamed this love would last
To wipe away those hurts of the past
As he'd said, till he left me broken

I had clung on to his band of promise
Even when I felt love had gone amiss
I missed seeing there was someone new
Me, he now despised and I had no clue
No clue I had till he left me broken

He now hated all that he'd eve loved
Loved about me as I was his beloved
Now I'm all alone, dreams gone past
Through he'd promised I'll be his last
His last I was, till he left me broken

A HUE OF BLUE

Like a kid, her eyes were brazen bright
With blooming thrills for an adventure
A fairytale trip to that promised bliss
For her heart, she'd given for ever after
Till you ran a pin along her stockings

In the warmth of her heart, you found
A sturdy partner who kept you afloat
En route to the shore of wonderment
Shining bright, the gleam of your torch
Till you ripped her sail of trust apart

In her arms you found graven loyalty
In a token of promise, she'll be the one
After the storms to wear your crown
She trailed the lead to your strangeness
Till your drought ate her ear of hope

Her childish exuberance lay bruised
Through those deep melancholic blues
Left upon the rolling waves to nowhere

She gazed at the ebbing tide of passion
Her tears shining through a hue of blue

DETERMINATION

Ambition is such a heady drug
Painting success in inviting hues
Act on to transport that ambition
It dies sometimes on its bed of conception
Or perish in a stillborn's plight

Determination defeats fear of risks
Or seeming barrenness of the plot
Bear your instincts and plough on
See the harvests in the mind's eye
With your heart and soul plodding

Patience and hard work can turn
Impossibilities into fertile ground
Making that seed sowed in hope
Sprout into greatness glowing out
Of what should have hindered it

I'LL LIVE

It's forbidden, that I should drown in sorrow's seas

When even on a rotting raft, I rather can stay afloat

I'll ne'er dust my shoes before my train's whistling pleas

When I leave, akin to a valiant soldier I would, in courage's coat

Those days of bewilderment, I've left behind

There then life and love played me like a pawn

When the sun came out and I was no more blind

I was grateful to welcome a brand new dawn

I would never pack up to halfway meet my end

Like a coward fleeing life's changing seasons

Here, baggage and all waiting for the next bend

But ne'er goodbye in a suicide note, for one too many reasons

ENIGMA

Her heart drums a warrior's song
Life is beautiful but no bed of hay
She swore to conquer as it comes
An unwavering stance, unhindered
Poised to take on giant shadows
The underdog has been unleashed

She is strong, a paragon of courage
Like quicksilver, she's turned elusive
Saddled on faith and belted in grace
Escaping all weights of their bigotry
Arching from her quiver of surprises
Under gazes of awe, she leapt forth

BRIDE OF THE MOON

Under the sky's canopy stood
A lady in such a flighty mood
Skittish and unstable
To hide her pain, she's unable

She gazed up at the moonlit sky
Under her umbrella held high
Sparkling in a flowing gown
She posed heralding her crown

Her jewels, a dream of fashion
Like a bride, she was clad with passion
Since the day she waited in vain
Her groom to come kiss her again

He'd left her in a full moon night
A search brought him not in sight
Since then on every full moon night
Aloof she would dress waiting for her knight

A BRIGHTER WORLD

I wonder if it's only in my mind
Or do you see it too?

The light beams brighter
When we reach out to the other

All that lies between us
Is a fickle line of indifference hovering o'er our hearts

Could we but strive a little harder
To reach out to the other all the while

We all are only a hand away
From lighting up the whole world

IT'S A POET'S LIFE

Needles in my pillow

Night's clad in sheens

Cup after cup of the brew

Still nowhere near the top

Words, imageries, rhythms

Flapping inside my head

Stop, I must and do its bid

To write that story

Of love, pain and injustice

Of comfort, belief and hope

Restless me, if I yield not

What would I do without you,

Poetry dear?

HUES OF THE RAINBOW

Between darkness' teeth
She made her crown fit
Reigning queen of solemn verses
Tuning her heart on sweet melodies

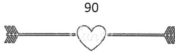

VIRTUAL LOVERS

I sit hoping that by the time this is through
We'll both be clear to what we are true
Knowing there's a name for everything
Even if not always what we would think

We argued this love was not designed
But agreed yielding would be unkind
Then we had to battle through a name
For our passions stood fertile in the game

When we spoke of our expectations
We agreed there would be limitations
As it would never be the normal kind
And on this one, we were candidly blind

How our love roams freely on virtuality
Unhindered, had we decide on actuality
Unbounded by the selfish need to pretend
To lure in any way until the dead end

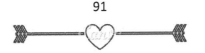

SWEET WHISPERS

Feel the sweetness of my tempest
Raging eagerness, it's a storm
Oh, come darling
Come hide in my love

This rush of sweetest joy
Feels like home's surest warmth
Heaven must be now

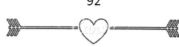

PHENOMENAL ME

Looking back never turned me into a pillar of salt

For piles of tastelessness, I'd left behind

Piles of bad investments, I'd left behind

Piles of resounding negativity, I'd left behind

Piles of condemnations for breaking all norms

Of their social barriers, I'd left behind

Piles of brokenheartedness and myopic, I'd left behind

Piles and piles of insecurities I'd left behind

I'm moving up the ladder of success

Erected on the ashes of all my insecurities

I'm moving onto new opportunities

A new lease of life for phenomenal me

MAGIC KISS

Your lips hold the secret
To my joy's completeness
There's magic in your kiss
I will never wish to miss

Put your arms around me
And never set me free
If death
Should come calling out to me
Let it find me
On your love's high beat

TRUE LOVE

Through lingering twists and wrong bends

Blinded by shadows along lonely paths

Slipping down slopes of disbelief

Crashing hopelessly at dead ends

Scaling walls of betrayals

Sounds of false alarms quietly deafening

Heartbreaking reverses to hopelessness

All in the labyrinthine pursuit of true love

TONIGHT (2)

There's magic in the air tonight
And we are in the warmth of our cuddles
Our love's been a warm ray of light
We get high on sun, fun, mirth and bubbles

My teddy bear wears no price tag
He bears a charm that is priceless
He neither snaps nor does he nag
His passion for love runs endless

Let the birds sing to the flowers
In their head dance to the wind
 Let the rain bathe in its showers
We'd stay all loved up in our bind

A hot mix of love and chocolates
Lavender baths, scented candles
This fusion of the best of mates
The urge for romance rekindles

CHILDHOOD

Our early years are like windows
Brace them well, firm and sturdy
Hinged unto guidance and care
As guards against flighty peers
Left loosely open, lose the child
To the raging winds of curiosity
To explore all unfolding scenes
Acted by adults and peers alike

HE HAD TO GO

Once fooled by his hugs of deceit
In his cold clutch, she found defeat
Through her every attempt to show
They could still make their love grow
His cheating ways, his lying heart
The wild beasts that tore her apart
But there was her still holding on
In spite of the hurt she had borne

Years went and left her very fraught
Of her pains and fears she said naught
But prayed this hurt would fly away
When her worth was on the sway
She needed peace and a clean break
From here she had to make a qauick streak
Or watch him walk away from her
To find her way after the burr

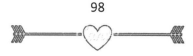

WITH ALL MY HEART

My heart lay quilted in patches
A fresh lease on life now taken
Strings of sad verses lie in batches
My life's dreams lay unshaken
This, I wish you to understand

Being happy is my first desire
Though I love you with all my heart
And my desire burns like a fire
Wishing we'll never have to part
So let's live as in wonderland

A BOND SO STRONG

This, I wish you would believe

Was dreamed in wonderland

When dark clouds I did see

I took trips of wish in mind

To be loved as I was

In spite of all my flaws

You and I are the best song

Heard from a heart in a distant while

So come and sing along

And to our fate reconcile

Now and ever after

Until thereafter

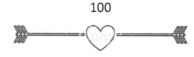

I SWEAR (2)

To your promise of forever
I swear, that trust I will revere
And give my heart now and ever
As our fates, we both discover
And to this oath, we stand under

You swear to mend my broken heart
Loving me through on to a new start
I vow if you've ever been hurt
I will rebuild your broken trust
From this pledge, may we never part

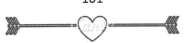

I BURN

With my head on your chest
Close to your heaving breast
Locked in your tight embrace
Is warmth none can replace
This slice of perfect bliss
Calm in love's chalice

Savoring your heady scent
To romance, I consent
From the edge of desire
My body's set on fire
That only you can quench
In your incense, let me burn

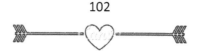

A SINGLE RED ROSE

Last night, I laid curled up in loneliness

Missing you and your tender loveliness

The sun smiled under the break of dawn

Then you came walking across the lawn

Bringing sweet fragrance into the room

Where I laid waiting as for my groom

A rose, a single red rose from my lover

The heat of passion again rising all over

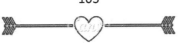

MEMORIES OF YOU

Being all by myself tonight
Memories of us so bright
Cocooned in our love den
Far from the world, hidden
Safe in our little heaven

I'm here thinking of you
And all those things we do
In the glow of our love
Gleaming like stars above
Love in our hearts lay graven
Images of when we were the other's idol

HONEY DROPS

My heart basks in glowing sunshine
The wind brushes your skin and mine
Your kisses taste like honey drops
Melting in my mouth like sweet pops

Love feeds me on hugs and kisses
Safe within your love embraces
With both our hearts singing a song
And lovebirds craving to dance along

Under the rising tides of evening heat
Another wave of passion had risen
Then into our love den we dive
To bring all our fantasies alive

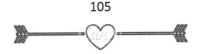

MAKE ME YOURS

You can see how always lonely I am without you
And it's all because of the beautiful things you do
Your love breathes life into the crannies of my soul
What will I do if this love should stop in its roll

Mesmerized by the tenderness of your love and care
I would wish with another I'll never have to share
Make me yours now, and forever be all just mine
I promise my heart and all of me will be all thine

With us together, the future promises to be bright
Your happiness would always be my delight
From now unto eternity, life will never be dull
For the syncing of our hearts will never call a lull

LOVE THAT IS EVERGREEN

Your dewdrops revived
the wilted petals of my prime

You are my rainbow
sending rays of hope to my heart

I smile at thunderstorms
For my heart is full of thoughts they bring of you

Your touch on my skin
Your taste in my mouth
Makes me happy to be a woman
Your woman
Your queen
Your lover

My mouth tasted
something sweeter than chocolate
something smoother than honey
when you first kissed me

If chocolates grew on trees
You will be that tree
And I will tend you with my life
For your love to be evergreen

I'm like marshmallow
To be taken at your pleasure
And when you reach out for me
My senses desert me
And I am lost in sweetness

Your silken voice
Sends oily thrills
Moisturizing the dryland
Of my harmattan

Your love
brings pagan thoughts
of making your body my shrine
to offer myself
to your naked desires

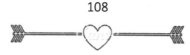

COURAGE

Beneath that giant pose

Lies the heart of an angel

With wings clipped in pain

If courage was to vanish

More hearts will perish

For them, for her

She smiled

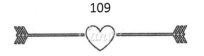

PUPPY LOVE

A journey back to love's Eden
Where we discovered bliss
Frolicking in the lush foliage
Of our teenage curiosity
Urged on by nature's thrills

Coy smiles, stolen kisses
Scared, the serpent may awake
The cursed fruit, we left whole

Teenage freshness lost
On sands of time and care
If fate but should concur
Lost years would wash away
To create our future's will

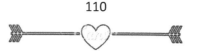

EVEN THE DEAD GETS FLOWERS

Between here and there lay
Tiny pieces of broken hearts
Lonely souls bask in longing
Layers of dried tears, choking
Hope rotting like wilted petals
No bouquet for their troubles
Even the dead gets flowers

Soaking in memories of yore
Chocolate wraps and choices
Beach walks and slow dances
Dreamy looks, sweet dreams
Under cherry strewn duvets
Late mornings, coffee in bed
Lazy smiles and shower games

Step out from your past, breathe
Embrace the emptiness
Sniff your favourite fragrance
Step into the sunshine, smile

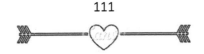

Walk along with your shadow

Buy yourself your best flowers

For even the dead gets flowers

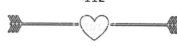

SWEET LOVE

When into your willing arms I run
I know solace is not very far
My heartbeats sync with yours
I bury my head in your calm
Free to be like a child, to be a woman
To be human, to be alive and love

I wink into your understanding eyes
As I wriggle well into another realm
To be the real me, anyone, anything
Freedom to walk, run, crawl or fly
Into open skies, surfing the clouds
Holding tight unto the tail of fantasy

Gliding onto ecstasy, the ultimate
In a tight hold, locked in your beauty
Dear sweet fantasy

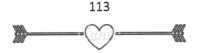

FADED MELODY

My heart wore a tear today
When a shadow of yesterday
Floated across the rafters
Of my ever cherished haven

I struggled to recall the lyrics
Of a once perfect melody
Strangely the rhythm returned
Like one tired from a journey

Then I stumbled on a memory
You had spoken those words
For words were all you had
Words I strung into a love song

My heart sings a new melody
To someone who sings along
So stranger, you better believe
My teardrops were of the moment

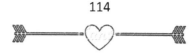

THE LONER'S JOURNEY

Embarking on a loner's journey
Soaring on the wings of slumber
Sojourner in the realm of spirits
Lured by the familiar or strange

Swinging between two worlds
Neither here nor there in totality
Being all you ever thought or not
From the chamber of your mind

Floating by like a celestial being
Watching allies turn feared foes
Foes offering bouquets of love
Altering pages in a mind's diary

Exiting the deep in the pristine
Pregnant with tales to tell or not
Memories left in ashes of dreams
Never resurrect in a gossip's tale

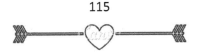

FROZEN TEARS

Once upon a broken heart
Hurt in distress she cried
Trust she bore now broken
Faith and hope stood away

Once upon a broken heart
Broken and tossed she was
Rife were tales of her woes
Being bitten twice, she wept

Once upon a broken heart
Smiles veiled frozen tears
Under their knowing looks
She dared to find herself

Once upon a broken heart
She saw a glimpse of hope
Naysayers watched in awe
As she turned out just fine

O' EARTH

Wallowing in the pit end of anxiety
Clad in nakedness of dying hopes
The moon loses its gaiety
When my gaze showers its face
O' earth, save me now or I perish!

Gloom veils me like a second skin
Pulled so thin it shows their scorn
Clinging to my body like nodules
Cursed to live like an untouchable
Come earth, rise up and save me!

Burning hate has scaled me raw
My friends have left with the wind
Leaving me in the grip of adversity
With only my voice to echo my pain
O' earth, rise up and embrace me!

MY NEW SCREENSAVER

Dark images menacing on my screen
Taking an aim at the gleam in my eyes
Not knowing how far my inner eye sees
And dares to read beyond the obvious
Chancing on grace to rewrite my story

Recharging life, overwriting sadness
Converting full stops to smart pauses
Editing impossibilities to possibilities
Deleting files on failures and self-loath
Surfing waves with a renewed resolve

Painting mirth into empty fields
Embracing popups of victorious songs
The cheeky smiley is let on the loose
A rainbow of trophies for battles won
Moonwalking on my new screensaver

ABOUT THE AUTHOR

Samuella J. Conteh is a prize-winning poet who has been published extensively in anthologies around the world. She has had many awards conferred on her, including Medal of Ambassador of Literature (AOL), World Poetic Star, Award of Mahatma Medal, Order of Shakespeare Medal (OOS), Premio Mundial a la Excellencies Literaria, 2019-2020 by the Government of Peru. She is a member of the Sierra Leone Writers Forum and board member of PEN-SL. Samuella is a mother and grandmother.

Published by Poetry Planet Publishing House

Designed by Tess Ritumalta

Cover picture artwork credit -   canva

Pictures used are taken in Pinterest and may contain its own copyrights

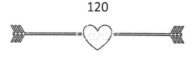

Printed in Great Britain
by Amazon